THE LIFE AND TEACHINGS OF THOTH HERMES TRISMEGISTUS

MANLY PALMER HALL

INTRODUCTION

THUNDER *rolled, lightning flashed, the veil of the Temple was rent from top to bottom. The venerable initiator, in his robes of blue and gold, slowly raised his jeweled wand and pointed with it into the darkness revealed by the tearing of the silken curtain: "Behold the Light of Egypt!" The candidate, in his plain white robe, gazed into the utter blackness framed by the two great Lotus-headed columns between which the veil had hung. As he watched, a luminous haze distributed itself throughout the atmosphere until the air was a mass of shining particles. The face of the neophyte was illumined by the soft glow as he scanned the shimmering cloud for some tangible object. The initiator spoke again: "This Light which ye behold is the secret luminance of the Mysteries. Whence it comes none knoweth, save the 'Master of the Light.' Behold Him!" Suddenly, through the gleaming mist a figure appeared, surrounded by a flickering greenish sheen. The initiator lowered his wand and, bowing his head, placed one hand edgewise against his breast in humble salutation. The neophyte stepped back in awe, partly blinded by the glory of the revealed figure. Gaining courage, the youth gazed again at the Divine One. The Form before him was considerably larger than that of a mortal man. The body seemed partly transparent so that the heart and brain could be seen*

INTRODUCTION

pulsating and radiant. As the candidate watched, the heart changed into an ibis, and the brain into a flashing emerald. In Its hand this mysterious Being bore a winged rod, entwined with serpents. The aged initiator, raising his wand, cried out in a loud voice: "All hail Thee, Thoth Hermes, Thrice Greatest; all hail Thee, Prince of Men; all hail Thee who standeth upon the head of Typhon!" At the same instant a lurid writhing dragon appeared--a hideous monster, part serpent, part crocodile, and part hog. From its mouth and nostrils poured sheets of flame and horrible sounds echoed through the vaulted chambers. Suddenly Hermes struck the advancing reptile with the serpent-wound staff and with snarling cry the dragon fell over upon its side, while the flames about it slowly died away. Hermes placed His foot upon the skull of the vanquished Typhon. The next instant, with a blaze of unbearable glory that sent the neophyte staggering backward against a pillar, the immortal Hermes, followed by streamers of greenish mist, passed through the chamber and faded into nothingness.

I
SUPPOSITIONS CONCERNING THE IDENTITY OF HERMES

Iamblichus averred that Hermes was the author of twenty thousand books; Manetho increased the number to more than thirty-six thousand (see James Gardner)--figures which make it evident that a solitary individual, even though he be overshadowed by divine prerogative, could scarcely have accomplished such a monumental labor. Among the arts and sciences which it is affirmed Hermes revealed to mankind were medicine, chemistry, law, arc, astrology, music, rhetoric, Magic, philosophy, geography, mathematics (especially geometry), anatomy, and oratory. Orpheus was similarly acclaimed by the Greeks.

In his *Biographia Antiqua*, Francis Barrett says of Hermes: "* * * if God ever appeared in man, he appeared in him, as is evident both from his books and his Pymander; in which works he has communicated the sum of the Abyss, and the divine knowledge to all posterity; by which he has demonstrated himself to have been not only an inspired divine, but also a deep philosopher, obtaining his wisdom from God and heavenly things, and not from man."

His transcendent learning caused Hermes to be identified with many of the early sages and prophets. In his Ancient Mythology, Bryant writes: "I have mentioned that Cadmus was the same as the Egyptian Thoth; and it is manifest from his being Hermes, and from the invention of letters being attributed to him. " (In the chapter on the theory of *Pythagorean Mathematics* will be found the table of the original Cadmean letters.) Investigators believe that it was Hermes who was known to the Jews as "Enoch," called by Kenealy the "Second Messenger of God." Hermes was accepted into the mythology of the Greeks, later becoming the Mercury of the Latins. He was revered through the form of the planet Mercury because this body is nearest to the sun: Hermes of all creatures was nearest to God, and became known as the Messenger of the Gods.

In the Egyptian drawings of him, Thoth carries a waxen writing tablet and serves as the recorder during the weighing of the souls of the dead in the judgment Hall of Osiris--a ritual of great significance. Hermes is of first importance to Masonic scholars, because he was the author of the Masonic initiatory rituals, which were borrowed from the Mysteries established by Hermes. Nearly all of the Masonic symbols are Hermetic in character. Pythagoras studied mathematics with the Egyptians and from them gained his knowledge of the symbolic geometric solids. Hermes is also revered for his reformation of the calendar system. He increased the year from 360 to 365 days, thus establishing a precedent which still prevails. The appellation "Thrice Greatest" was given to Hermes because he was considered the greatest of all philosophers, the greatest of all priests, and the greatest of all kings. It is worthy of note that the last poem of America's beloved poet, Henry Wadsworth Longfellow, was a lyric ode to Hermes. (See *Chambers' Encyclopædia*.)

2
THE MUTILATED HERMETIC FRAGMENTS

On the subject of the Hermetic books, James Campbell Brown, in his *History of Chemistry*, has written: "Leaving the Chaldean and earliest Egyptian periods, of which we have remains but no record, and from which no names of either chemists or philosophers have come down to us, we now approach the Historic Period, when books were written, not at first upon parchment or paper, but upon papyrus. A series of early Egyptian books is attributed to Hermes Trismegistus, who may have been a real *savant*, or may be a personification of a long succession of writers. * * * He is identified by some with the Greek god Hermes, and the Egyptian Thoth or Tuti, who was the moon-god, and is represented in ancient paintings as ibis-headed with the disc and crescent of the moon. The Egyptians regarded him as the god of wisdom, letters, and the recording of time. It is in consequence of the great respect entertained for Hermes by the old alchemists that chemical writings were called 'hermetic,' and that the phrase 'hermetically sealed' is still in use to designate the closing of a glass vessel by fusion, after the manner of chemical manipulators. We find the same root in the hermetic medicines of Paracelsus, and the hermetic freemasonry of the Middle Ages."

Among the fragmentary writings believed to have come from the stylus of Hermes are two famous works. The first is the *Emerald Table*, and the second is the *Divine Pymander*, or, as it is more commonly called, *The Shepherd of Men*, a discussion of which follows. One outstanding point in connection with Hermes is that he was one of the few philosopher-priests of pagandom upon whom the early Christians did not vent their spleen. Some Church Fathers went so far as to declare that Hermes exhibited many symptoms of intelligence, and that if he had only been born in a more enlightened age so that he might have benefited by *their* instructions he would have been a really great man!

HERMES MERCURIUS TRISMEGISTUS.

THE LIFE AND TEACHINGS OF THOTH HERMES TRISMEGISTUS

IN HIS *STROMATA*, CLEMENT OF ALEXANDRIA, ONE OF THE FEW chroniclers of pagan lore whose writings have been preserved to this age, gives practically all the information that is known concerning the original forty-two books of Hermes and the importance with which these books were regarded by both the temporal and spiritual powers of Egypt. Clement describes one of their ceremonial processions as follows:

"For the Egyptians pursue a philosophy of their own. This is principally shown by their sacred ceremonial. For first advances the Singer, bearing some one of the symbols of music. For they say that he must learn two of the books of Hermes, the one of which contains the hymns of the gods, the second the regulations for the king's life. And after the Singer advances the Astrologer, with a horologe in his hand, and a palm, the symbols of astrology. He must have the astrological books of Hermes, which are four in number, always in his mouth. Of these, one is about the order of the fixed stars that are visible, and another about the conjunctions and luminous appearances of the sun and moon; and the rest respecting their risings. Next in order advances the sacred Scribe, with wings on his head, and in his hand a book and rule, in which were writing ink and the reed, with which they write. And he must be acquainted with what are called hieroglyphics, and know about cosmography and geography, the position of the sun and moon, and about the five planets; also the description of Egypt, and the chart of the Nile; and the description of the equipment of the priests and of the place consecrated to them, and about the measures and the things in use in the sacred rites. Then the Stole-keeper follows those previously mentioned, with the cubit of justice and the cup for libations. He is acquainted with all points called Pædeutic (relating to training) and Moschophaltic (sacrificial). There are also ten books which relate to the honour paid by them to their gods, and containing the Egyptian worship; as that relating to sacrifices, first-fruits, hymns, prayers, processions, festivals, and the like. And behind all walks the Prophet, with the water-vase carried openly in his arms; who is followed by those who carry the issue of loaves. He, as being the governor of the temple, learns the ten books called 'Hieratic'; and they contain all about the laws, and the gods, and the whole of the training of the priests. For the Prophet is, among the Egyptians, also over the distribution of the revenues. There are then forty-two books of Hermes indispensably necessary; of which the six-and-thirty containing the whole philosophy of the Egyptians are learned by the forementioned personages; and the other six, which are medical, by the Pastophoroi (image-bearers),--treating of the structure of the body, and of disease, and instruments, and medicines, and about the eyes, and the last about women.

One of the greatest tragedies of the philosophic world was the loss of nearly all of the forty-two books of Hermes mentioned in the foregoing. These books disappeared during the burning of Alexandria, for the Romans--and later the Christians--realized that until these books were eliminated they could never bring the Egyptians into subjection. The volumes which escaped the fire were buried in the desert and their location is now known to only a few initiates of the secret schools.

3

THE BOOK OF THOTH

While Hermes still walked the earth with men, he entrusted to his chosen successors the sacred *Book of Thoth*. This work contained the secret processes by which the regeneration of humanity was to be accomplished and also served as the key to his other writings. Nothing definite is known concerning the contents of the *Book of Thoth* other than that its pages were covered with strange hieroglyphic figures and symbols, which gave to those acquainted with their use unlimited power over the spirits of the air and the subterranean divinities. When certain areas of the brain are stimulated by the secret processes of the Mysteries, the consciousness of man is extended and he is permitted to behold the Immortals and enter into the presence of the superior gods. The *Book of Thoth* described the method whereby this stimulation was accomplished. In truth, therefore, it was the "Key to Immortality."

According to legend, the *Book of Thoth* was kept in a golden box in the inner sanctuary of the temple. There was but one key and this was in the possession of the "Master of the Mysteries," the highest initiate of the Hermetic Arcanum. He alone knew what was written in the secret book. The *Book of Thoth* was lost to the ancient world with the decay of the Mysteries, but its faithful initiates carried it sealed in the sacred casket into another land. The book is still in existence and continues to lead the disciples of this age into the presence of the Immortals. No other information can be given to the world concerning it now, but the apostolic succession from the first hierophant initiated by Hermes himself remains unbroken to this day, and those who are peculiarly fitted to serve the Immortals may discover this priceless document if they will search sincerely and tirelessly for it.

It has been asserted that the *Book of Thoth* is, in reality, the mysterious *Tarot* of the Bohemians--a strange emblematic book of seventy-eight leaves which has been in possession of the gypsies since the time when they were driven from their ancient temple, the Serapeum. (According to the Secret Histories the gypsies were originally Egyptian priests.) There are now in the world several secret schools privileged to initiate candidates into the Mysteries, but in nearly every instance they lighted their altar fires from the flaming torch of *Herm*. Hermes in his *Book of Thoth* revealed to all mankind the "One Way," and for ages the wise of every nation and every faith have reached immortality by the "Way" established by Hermes in the midst of the darkness for the redemption of humankind.

4
POIMANDRES, THE VISION OF HERMES

The *Divine Pymander of Hermes Mercurius Trismegistus* is one of the earliest of the Hermetic writings now extant. While probably not in its original form, having been remodeled during the first centuries of the Christian Era and incorrectly translated since, this work undoubtedly contains many of the original concepts of the Hermetic cultus. *The Divine Pymander* consists of seventeen fragmentary writings gathered together and put forth as one work. The second book of *The Divine Pymander*, called *Poimandres*, or *The Vision*, is believed to describe the method by which the divine wisdom was first revealed to Hermes. It was after Hermes had received this revelation that he began his ministry, teaching to all who would listen the secrets of the invisible universe as they had been unfolded to him.

The Vision is the most famous of all the Hermetic fragments, and contains an exposition of Hermetic cosmogony and the secret sciences of the Egyptians regarding the culture and unfoldment of the human soul. For some time it was erroneously called "The Genesis of Enoch," but that mistake has now been rectified. At hand while preparing the following interpretation of the symbolic philosophy concealed within *The Vision of Hermes* the present author has had these reference works: *The Divine Pymander of Hermes Mercurius Trismegistus* (London, 1650), translated out of the Arabic and Greek by Dr. Everard; *Hermetica* (Oxford, 1924), edited by Walter Scott; *Hermes, The Mysteries of Egypt* (Philadelphia, 1925), by Edouard Schure; and the *Thrice-Greatest Hermes* (London, 1906), by G. R. S. Mead. To the material contained in the above volumes he has added commentaries based upon the esoteric philosophy of the ancient Egyptians, together with amplifications derived partly from other Hermetic fragments and partly from the secret arcanum of the Hermetic sciences. For the sake of clarity, the narrative form has been chosen in preference to the original dialogic style, and obsolete words have given place to those in current use.

Hermes, while wandering in a rocky and desolate place, gave himself over to meditation and prayer. Following the secret instructions of the Temple, he gradually freed his higher consciousness from the bondage of his bodily senses; and, thus released, his divine nature revealed to him the mysteries of the transcendental spheres. He beheld a figure, terrible and awe-inspiring. It was the Great Dragon, with wings stretching across the sky and light streaming in all directions from its body. (The Mysteries taught that the Universal Life was personified as a dragon.) The Great Dragon called Hermes by name, and asked him why he thus meditated upon the World Mystery. Terrified by the spectacle, Hermes prostrated himself before the Dragon, beseeching it to reveal its identity. The great creature answered that it was *Poimandres*, the *Mind of the Universe*, the Creative Intelligence, and the Absolute Emperor of all. (Schure identifies Poimandres as the god Osiris.) Hermes then besought Poimandres to disclose the nature of the universe and the constitution of the gods. The Dragon acquiesced, bidding Trismegistus hold its image in his mind.

THOTH, THE IBIS HEADED.

IMMEDIATELY THE FORM OF POIMANDRES CHANGED. WHERE IT had stood there was a glorious and pulsating Radiance. This Light was the spiritual nature of the Great Dragon itself. Hermes was "raised" into the midst of this Divine Effulgence and the universe of material things faded from his consciousness.

Presently a great darkness descended and, expanding, swallowed up the Light. Everything was troubled. About Hermes swirled a mysterious watery substance which gave forth a smokelike vapor. The air was filled with inarticulate moanings and sighings which seemed to come from the Light swallowed up in the darkness. His mind told Hermes that the Light was the form of the spiritual universe and that the swirling darkness which had engulfed it represented material substance.

Then out of the imprisoned Light a mysterious and Holy Word came forth and took its stand upon the smoking waters. This Word--the Voice of the Light--rose out of the darkness as a great pillar, and the fire and the air followed after it, but the earth and the water remained unmoved below. Thus the waters of Light were divided from the waters of darkness, and from the waters of Light were formed the worlds above and from the waters of darkness were formed the worlds below. The earth and the water next mingled, becoming inseparable, and the Spiritual Word which is called *Reason* moved upon their surface, causing endless turmoil.

Then again was heard the voice of Poimandres, but His form was not revealed: "I Thy God am the Light and the Mind which were before substance was divided from spirit and darkness from Light. And the Word which appeared as a pillar of flame out of the darkness is the Son of God, born of the mystery of the Mind. The name of that Word is *Reason*. Reason is the offspring of Thought and Reason shall divide the Light from the darkness and establish Truth in the midst of the waters. Understand, O Hermes, and meditate deeply upon the mystery. That which in you sees and hears is not of the earth, but is the Word of God incarnate. So it is said that Divine Light dwells in the midst of mortal darkness, and ignorance cannot divide them. The union of the Word and the Mind produces that mystery which is called

Life. As the darkness without you is divided against itself, so the darkness within you is likewise divided. The Light and the fire which rise are the divine man, ascending in the path of the Word, and that which fails to ascend is the mortal man, which may not partake of immortality. Learn deeply of the Mind and its mystery, for therein lies the secret of immortality."

The Dragon again revealed its form to Hermes, and for a long time the two looked steadfastly one upon the other, eye to eye, so that Hermes trembled before the gaze of Poimandres. At the Word of the Dragon the heavens opened and the innumerable Light Powers were revealed, soaring through Cosmos on pinions of streaming fire. Hermes beheld the spirits of the stars, the celestials controlling the universe, and all those Powers which shine with the radiance of the One Fire--the glory of the Sovereign Mind. Hermes realized that the sight which he beheld was revealed to him only because Poimandres had spoken a Word. The Word was Reason, and by the Reason of the Word invisible things were made manifest. Divine Mind--the Dragon--continued its discourse:

"Before the visible universe was formed its mold was cast. This mold was called the *Archetype*, and this Archetype was in the Supreme Mind long before the process of creation began. Beholding the Archetypes, the Supreme Mind became enamored with Its own thought; so, taking the Word as a mighty hammer, It gouged out caverns in primordial space and cast the form of the spheres in the Archetypal mold, at the same time sowing in the newly fashioned bodies the seeds of living things. The darkness below, receiving the hammer of the Word, was fashioned into an orderly universe. The elements separated into strata and each brought forth living creatures. The Supreme Being--the Mind--male and female, brought forth the Word; and the Word, suspended between Light and darkness, was delivered of another Mind called the *Workman*, the *Master-Builder*, or the *Maker of Things*.

"In this manner it was accomplished, O Hermes: The Word moving like a breath through space called forth the *Fire* by the friction of its motion. Therefore, the Fire is called the *Son of Striving*. The Workman passed as a whirlwind through the universe, causing the substances to vibrate and glow with its friction, The Son of Striving thus formed *Seven Governors*, the Spirits of the Planets, whose orbits bounded the world; and the Seven Governors controlled the world by the mysterious power called *Destiny* given them by the Fiery Workman. When the *Second Mind* (The Workman) had organized Chaos, the Word of God rose straightway our of its prison of substance, leaving the elements without Reason, and joined Itself to the nature of the Fiery Workman. Then the Second Mind, together with the risen Word, established Itself in the midst of the universe and whirled the wheels of the Celestial Powers. This shall continue from an infinite beginning to an infinite end, for the beginning and the ending are in the same place and state.

"Then the downward-turned and unreasoning elements brought forth creatures without Reason. Substance could not bestow Reason, for Reason had ascended out of it. The air produced flying things and the waters such as swim. The earth conceived strange four-footed and creeping beasts, dragons, composite demons, and grotesque monsters. Then the Father--the Supreme Mind--being Light and Life, fashioned a glorious Universal Man in Its own image, not an earthy man but a heavenly Man dwelling in the Light of God. The *Supreme Mind* loved the Man It had fashioned and delivered to Him the control of the creations and workmanships.

"The Man, desiring to labor, took up His abode in the sphere of generation and observed the works of His brother--the Second Mind--which sat upon the Ring of the Fire. And having beheld the achievements of the Fiery Workman, He willed also to make things, and His Father gave permission. The Seven Governors, of whose powers He partook, rejoiced and each gave the Man a share of Its own nature.

"The Man longed to pierce the circumference of the circles and understand the mystery of Him who sat upon the Eternal Fire. Having already all power, He stooped down and peeped through the seven Harmonies and, breaking through the strength of the circles, made Himself manifest to Nature stretched out below. The Man, looking into the depths, smiled, for He beheld a shadow upon the earth and a likeness mirrored in the waters, which shadow and likeness were a reflection of Himself. The Man fell in love with His own shadow and desired to descend into it. Coincident with the desire, the Intelligent Thing united Itself with the unreasoning image or shape.

"Nature, beholding the descent, wrapped herself about the Man whom she loved, and the two were mingled. For this reason, earthy man is composite. Within him is the Sky Man, immortal and beautiful; without is Nature, mortal and destructible. Thus, suffering is the result of the Immortal Man's falling in love with His shadow and giving up Reality to dwell in the darkness of illusion; for, being immortal, man has the power of the Seven Governors--also the Life, the Light, and the Word-but being mortal, he is controlled by the Rings of the Governors--Fate or Destiny.

"Of the Immortal Man it should be said that He is hermaphrodite, or male and female, and eternally watchful. He neither slumbers nor sleeps, and is governed by a Father also both male and female, and ever watchful. Such is the mystery kept hidden to this day, for Nature, being mingled in marriage with the Sky Man, brought forth a wonder most wonderful--seven men, all bisexual, male and female, and upright of stature, each one exemplifying the natures of the Seven Governors. These O Hermes, are the seven races, species, and wheels.

"After this manner were the seven men generated. Earth was the female element and water the male element, and from the fire and the æther they received their spirits, and Nature produced bodies after the species and shapes of men. And man received the Life and Light of the Great Dragon, and of the Life was made his Soul and of the Light his Mind. And so, all these composite creatures containing immortality, but partaking of mortality, continued in this state for the duration of a period. They reproduced themselves out of themselves, for each was male and female. But at the end of the period the knot of Destiny was untied by the will of God and the bond of all things was loosened.

"Then all living creatures, including man, which had been hermaphroditical, were separated, the males being set apart by themselves and the females likewise, according to the dictates of Reason.

"Then God spoke to the Holy Word within the soul of all things, saying: 'Increase in increasing and multiply in multitudes, all you, my creatures and workmanships. Let him that is endued with Mind know himself to be immortal and that the cause of death is the love of the body; and let him learn all things that are, for he who has recognized himself enters into the state of Good.'

A GREEK FORM OF HERMES.

"And when God had said this, Providence, with the aid of the Seven Governors and Harmony, brought the sexes together, making the mixtures and establishing the generations, and all things were multiplied according to their kind. He who through the error of attachment loves his body, abides wandering in darkness, sensible and suffering the things of death, but he who realizes that the body is but the tomb of his soul, rises to immortality."

Then Hermes desired to know why men should be deprived of immortality for the sin of ignorance alone. The Great Dragon answered:, To the ignorant the body is supreme and they are incapable of realizing the immortality that is within them. Knowing only the body which is subject to death, they believe in death because they worship that substance which is the cause and reality of death."

Then Hermes asked how the righteous and wise pass to God, to which Poimandres replied: "That which the Word of God said, say I: 'Because the Father of all things consists of Life and Light, whereof man is made.' If, therefore, a man shall learn and understand the nature of Life and Light, then he shall pass into the eternity of Life and Light."

Hermes next inquired about the road by which the wise attained to Life eternal, and Poimandres continued: "Let the man endued with a Mind mark, consider, and learn of himself, and with the power of his Mind divide himself from his not-self and become a servant of Reality."

Hermes asked if all men did not have Minds, and the Great Dragon replied: "Take heed what you say, for I am the Mind--the Eternal Teacher. I am the Father of the *Word*--the Redeemer of all men--and in the nature of the wise the Word takes flesh. By means of the Word, the world is saved. I, *Thought* (Thoth)--the Father of the Word, the Mind--come only unto men that are holy and good, pure and merciful, and that live piously and religiously, and my presence is an inspiration and a help to them, for when I come they immediately know all things and adore the Universal Father. Before such wise and philosophic ones die, they learn to renounce their senses, knowing that these are the enemies of their immortal souls.

"I will not permit the evil senses to control the bodies of those who love me, nor will I allow evil emotions and evil thoughts to enter them. I become as a porter or doorkeeper, and shut out evil, protecting the wise from their own lower nature. But to the wicked, the envious and the covetous, I come not, for such cannot understand the mysteries of *Mind*; therefore, I am unwelcome. I leave them to the avenging demon that they are making in their own souls, for evil each day increases itself and torments man more sharply, and each evil deed adds to the evil deeds that are gone before until finally evil destroys itself. The punishment of desire is the agony of unfulfillment."

Hermes bowed his head in thankfulness to the Great Dragon who had taught him so much, and begged to hear more concerning the ultimate of the human soul. So Poimandres resumed: "At death the material body of man is returned to the elements from which it came, and the invisible divine man ascends to the source from whence he came, namely the *Eighth Sphere*. The evil passes to the dwelling place of the demon, and the senses, feelings, desires, and body passions return to their source, namely the Seven Governors, whose natures in the lower man destroy but in the invisible spiritual man give life.

"After the lower nature has returned to the brutishness, the higher struggles again to regain its spiritual estate. It ascends the seven Rings upon which sit the Seven Governors and returns to each their lower powers in this manner: Upon the first ring sits the Moon, and to it is returned the ability to increase and diminish. Upon the second ring sits Mercury, and to it are returned machinations, deceit, and craftiness. Upon the third ring sits Venus, and to it are returned the lusts and passions. Upon the fourth ring sits the Sun, and to this Lord are returned ambitions. Upon the fifth ring sits Mars, and to it are returned rashness and profane boldness. Upon the sixth ring sits Jupiter, and to it are returned the sense of accumulation and riches. And upon the seventh ring sits Saturn, at the Gate of Chaos, and to it are returned falsehood and evil plotting.

"Then, being naked of all the accumulations of the seven Rings, the soul comes to the Eighth Sphere, namely, the ring of the fixed stars. Here, freed of all illusion, it dwells in the Light and sings praises to the Father in a voice which only the pure of spirit may understand. Behold, O Hermes, there is a great mystery in the Eighth Sphere, for the Milky Way is the seed-ground of souls, and from it they drop into the Rings, and to the Milky Way they return again from the wheels of Saturn. But some cannot climb the seven-runged ladder of the Rings. So they wander in darkness below and are swept into eternity with the illusion of sense and earthiness.

"The path to immortality is hard, and only a few find it. The rest await the Great Day when the wheels of the universe shall be stopped and the immortal sparks shall escape from the sheaths of substance. Woe unto those who wait, for they must return again, unconscious and unknowing, to the seed-ground of stars, and await a new beginning. Those who are saved by the light of the mystery which I have revealed unto you, O Hermes, and which I now bid you to establish among men, shall return again to the Father who dwelleth in the White Light, and shall deliver themselves up to the Light and shall be absorbed into the Light, and in the Light they shall become Powers in God. This is the Way of *Good* and is revealed only to them that have wisdom.

"Blessed art thou, O Son of Light, to whom of all men, I, Poimandres, the Light of the World, have revealed myself. I order you to go forth, to become as a guide to those who wander in darkness, that all men within whom dwells the spirit of *My Mind* (The Universal Mind) may be saved by My Mind in you, which shall call forth My Mind in them. Establish My Mysteries and they shall not fail from the earth, for I am the Mind of the Mysteries and until Mind fails (which is never) my Mysteries cannot fail." With these parting words, Poimandres, radiant with celestial light, vanished, mingling with the powers of the heavens. Raising his eyes unto the heavens, Hermes blessed the

Father of All Things and consecrated his life to the service of the Great Light.

Thus preached Hermes: "O people of the earth, men born and made of the elements, but with the spirit of the Divine Man within you, rise from your sleep of ignorance! Be sober and thoughtful. Realize that your home is not in the earth but in the Light. Why have you delivered yourselves over unto death, having power to partake of immortality? Repent, and *change your minds*. Depart from the dark light and forsake corruption forever. Prepare yourselves to climb through the Seven Rings and to blend your souls with the eternal Light."

Some who heard mocked and scoffed and went their way, delivering themselves to the Second Death from which there is no salvation. But others, casting themselves before the feet of Hermes, besought him to teach them the Way of Life. He lifted them gently, receiving no approbation for himself, and staff in hand, went forth teaching and guiding mankind, and showing them how they might be saved. In the worlds of men, Hermes sowed the seeds of wisdom and nourished the seeds with the Immortal Waters. And at last came the evening of his life, and as the brightness of the light of earth was beginning to go down, Hermes commanded his disciples to preserve his doctrines inviolate throughout all ages. The *Vision of Poimandres* he committed to writing that all men desiring immortality might therein find the way.

In concluding his exposition of the *Vision*, Hermes wrote: "The sleep of the body is the sober watchfulness of the Mind and the shutting of my eyes reveals the true Light. My silence is filled with budding life and hope, and is full of good. My words are the blossoms of fruit of the tree of my soul. For this is the faithful account of what I received from my true Mind, that is Poimandres, the Great Dragon, the Lord of the Word, through whom I became inspired by God with the Truth. Since that day my Mind has been ever with me and in my own soul it hath given birth to the Word: the Word is Reason, and Reason hath redeemed me. For which cause, with all my soul and all my strength, I give praise and blessing unto God the Father, the Life and the Light, and the Eternal Good.

"Holy is God, the Father of all things, the One who is before the First Beginning.

"Holy is God, whose will is performed and accomplished by His own Powers which He hath given birth to out of Himself.

"Holy is God, who has determined that He shall be known, and who is known by His own to whom He reveals Himself.

"Holy art Thou, who by Thy Word (Reason) hast established all things.

"Holy art Thou, of whom all Nature is the image.

"Holy art Thou, whom the inferior nature has not formed.

"Holy art Thou, who art stronger than all powers.

"Holy art Thou, who art greater than all excellency.

"Holy art Thou, who art better than all praise.

"Accept these reasonable sacrifices from a pure soul and a heart stretched out unto Thee.

"O Thou Unspeakable, Unutterable, to be praised with silence!

"I beseech Thee to look mercifully upon me, that I may not err from the knowledge of Thee and that I may enlighten those that are in ignorance, my brothers and Thy sons.

"Therefore I believe Thee and bear witness unto Thee, and depart in peace and in trustfulness into Thy Light and Life.

"Blessed art Thou, O Father! The man Thou hast fashioned would be sanctified with Thee as Thou hast given him power to sanctify others with Thy Word and Thy Truth."

The *Vision of Hermes*, like nearly all of the Hermetic writings, is an allegorical exposition of great philosophic and mystic truths, and its hidden meaning may be comprehended only by those who have been

www.ingramcontent.com/pod-product-compliance
Lightning Source LLC
Chambersburg PA
CBHW052208070526
44585CB00017B/2114